8/17

T 2021

THE WORLD'S WORST EARTHQUAKES

by John R. Baker

Raintree is an imprint of Capstone Global Library Limited, a company incorporated in England and Wales having its registered office at 264 Banbury Road, Oxford, OX2 7DY – Registered company number: 6695582

www.raintree.co.uk
myorders@raintree.co.uk

Edited by Aaron Sautter
Designed by Steve Mead
Picture research by Jo Miller
Production by Tori Abraham
Originated by Capstone Global Library Limited
Printed and bound in China

ISBN 978 1 474 72476 0 (hardback)
20 19 18 17 16
10 9 8 7 6 5 4 3 2 1

ISBN 978 1 474 72480 7 (paperback)
21 20 19 18 17
10 9 8 7 6 5 4 3 2 1

British Library Cataloguing in Publication Data
A full catalogue record for this book is available from the British Library.

Acknowledgements
We would like to thank the following for permission to reproduce photographs:
Corbis: Sygma/Sergio Dornates, 20–21; Getty Images: AFP/STF, 8–9, ChinaFotoPress/Yang Weihua, 16-17, Justin Sullivan, 28–29; Glow Images: Stock Connection/View Stock, 10–11; Newscom: ABACA/DPA, 12–13, akg-images, 24–25, EPA/Sergei Chirikov, 22–23, Reuters/Damir Sagolj, 26–27; Shutterstock: leonello calvetti, cover, 3, 31, SDubi, design elements, think4photop, cover, Tom Wang, 4–5, xpixel, design elements; Wikimedia: NARA/Chadwick, H.D., 14–15, UN Photo/Logan Abassi, 6-7, US Navy/PH2 Philip A. McDaniel, 18–19

Every effort has been made to contact copyright holders of material reproduced in this book. Any omissions will be rectified in subsequent printings if notice is given to the publisher.

CONTENTS

EARTH-SHAKING POWER

THE RICHTER SCALE

9.0+
8.0
7.0
6.0
5.0
4.0
3.0
2.0
0.0

The **magnitude** of an earthquake is measured using the Richter scale. Weak earthquakes have a low magnitude. Powerful earthquakes are rated at 7.0 or higher.

magnitude measure of the size of an earthquake

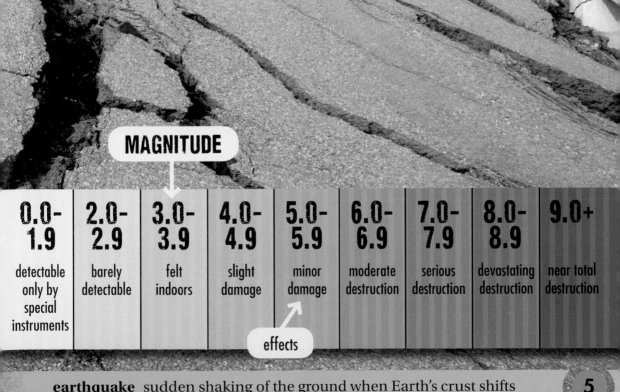

The ground rumbles and splits open. Bridges sway. Buildings topple. What's causing this destruction? An **earthquake**! These powerful ground-shaking events occur somewhere on Earth nearly every hour. Hold on tight. It's time to learn about the worst earthquakes in the world.

MAGNITUDE

0.0–1.9	2.0–2.9	3.0–3.9	4.0–4.9	5.0–5.9	6.0–6.9	7.0–7.9	8.0–8.9	9.0+
detectable only by special instruments	barely detectable	felt indoors	slight damage	minor damage	moderate destruction	serious destruction	devastating destruction	near total destruction

effects

earthquake sudden shaking of the ground when Earth's crust shifts

DISASTER IN HAITI

Location:
Port-au-Prince,
Haiti

Date:
12 January 2010

Rating:

9.0+
8.0
7.0 ◄
6.0
5.0
4.0
3.0
2.0
0.0

Haiti wasn't prepared for the major 7.0 earthquake that struck in 2010. The quake's **epicentre** was close to the city of Port-au-Prince. Thousands of buildings collapsed. More than 200,000 people died in the disaster.

Hundreds of thousands of people were left homeless after the Haiti earthquake. Many of the survivors were forced to live in tents.

epicentre point on Earth's surface directly above the place where an earthquake occurs

TOPPING THE SCALE

Location:
Chile

Date:
22 May 1960

Rating:

9.0+
8.0
7.0
6.0
5.0
4.0
3.0
2.0
0.0

On 22 May 1960, the strongest earthquake in history hit Chile. The quake measured an incredible 9.5 on the Richter scale. Three destructive **tsunamis** then slammed into Chile's coast. The disaster killed about 1,600 people.

About 16 earthquakes with a magnitude of 7.0 or greater occur around the world each year.

tsunami large, destructive ocean wave caused by an underwater earthquake, landslide or volcanic eruption

HISTORY'S DEADLIEST QUAKE

Location:
Shaanxi (Shensi), China

Date:
23 January 1556

Rating:

9.0+
8.0
7.0
6.0
5.0
4.0
3.0
2.0
0.0

The deadliest known earthquake occurred in China on 23 January 1556. The killer 8.0 quake claimed more than 830,000 lives. The huge earthquake also changed the land. Mountains crumbled. The paths of rivers changed. Major floods hit many areas.

Experts believe **liquefaction** caused much of the destruction in the 1556 earthquake. The quake caused loose soil under buildings to flow like a liquid. Buildings then toppled without solid ground beneath them.

liquefaction process of soil becoming fluid and unstable during an earthquake

NEPAL TRAGEDY

Location:
Nepal

Date:
25 April and
12 May 2015

Rating:

9.0+
8.0
7.0
6.0
5.0
4.0
3.0
2.0
0.0

On 25 April 2015, a 7.8 earthquake rocked Nepal. A 7.3-magnitude **aftershock** shook the area several days later. **Landslides** flattened entire villages. About 9,000 people died in the disaster. Hundreds of thousands more lost their homes.

aftershock smaller earthquake that follows a large one
landslide large mass of earth and rocks that suddenly slides down a mountain or hill

The first earthquake in Nepal shifted Mount Everest, the world's tallest mountain. It moved about 3 centimetres (1.2 inches) south-west.

SAN FRANCISCO DISASTER

Location:
San Francisco, California, USA

Date:
18 April 1906

Rating:

9.0+
8.0
7.0
6.0
5.0
4.0
3.0
2.0
0.0

A powerful 7.8 earthquake shook San Francisco, USA, in 1906. It crumbled houses and burst water mains. When fires broke out, firefighters didn't have enough water. The fires burned for two days. About 3,000 people died in the disaster.

FACT

San Francisco lies near the San Andreas **Fault**. During the 1906 earthquake, a fence on the fault broke in two. The two ends shifted about 5 metres (15 feet) apart.

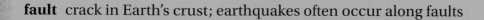

fault   crack in Earth's crust; earthquakes often occur along faults

CHINESE LANDSLIDES

Location:
Sichuan province,
China

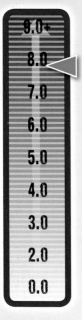

Date:
12 May 2008

Rating:

9.0+
8.0
7.0
6.0
5.0
4.0
3.0
2.0
0.0

China is often hit by large earthquakes. A 7.9-magnitude quake hit Sichuan **province** on 12 May 2008. More than 87,000 people died or went missing. Large landslides blocked the narrow mountain roads. The army sent helicopters to rescue survivors.

FACT

The landslides also blocked some rivers. Many lakes were formed. The largest threatened the homes of more than 1 million people. The government blasted through tonnes of rock to release the water.

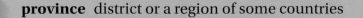

BOXING DAY TSUNAMI

Location:
Sumatra,
Indonesia

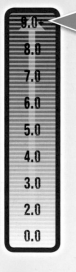

Date:
26 December 2004

Rating:

9.0
8.0
7.0
6.0
5.0
4.0
3.0
2.0
0.0

On 26 December 2004, a massive 9.1 earthquake hit near the coast of Sumatra, Indonesia. It created one of the deadliest tsunamis ever recorded. The killer wave reached up to 30 metres (100 feet) high. More than 220,000 people died or went missing.

FACT

The 2004 earthquake in Sumatra was the third-strongest ever recorded. It created a 1,500-kilometre (900-mile) crack along the ocean floor.

Location:
Mexico City,
Mexico

Date:
19 September
1985

Rating:

9.0+
8.0
7.0
6.0
5.0
4.0
3.0
2.0
0.0

A powerful 8.0 earthquake hit near Mexico City on 19 September 1985. The city's soft ground made the disaster worse. The quake's **seismic waves** easily toppled unsteady buildings. The disaster killed at least 9,500 people.

FACT

After the earthquake, Mexico's government passed laws to make sure new buildings were stronger.

TERROR IN TURKEY

Location:
Izmit, Turkey

Date:
17 August 1999

Rating:

9.0+
8.0
7.0
6.0
5.0
4.0
3.0
2.0
0.0

People in Izmit, Turkey, got a horrible shock on 17 August 1999. A 7.6-magnitude earthquake shook them awake in the middle of the night. Many buildings collapsed. The disaster killed at least 17,000 people. It injured another 50,000.

Around 500,000 people in Turkey lost their homes in the 1999 earthquake.

GOOD FRIDAY EARTHQUAKE

Location:

Prince William
Sound, Alaska

Date:

27 March 1964

Rating:

9.0+
8.0
7.0
6.0
5.0
4.0
3.0
2.0
0.0

The Alaskan earthquake caused a giant tsunami. The huge wave reached as far as Hawaii, where it claimed 113 lives.

The second-strongest earthquake ever recorded hit in 1964. On Good Friday, the 9.2 quake shook towns along Alaska's coast. Docks fell into the sea. Railway tracks were bent and twisted. Many buildings collapsed. Incredibly, only 15 people in Alaska died.

JAPANESE DISASTERS

Location:

Japan

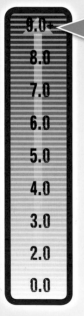

Date:

11 March 2011

Rating:

9.0+
8.0
7.0
6.0
5.0
4.0
3.0
2.0
0.0

On 11 March 2011 a massive 9.0-magnitude earthquake triggered a huge, 30-metre- (100-foot-) high tsunami in Japan. The giant wave then flooded a nuclear power plant. It caused a **meltdown**. These disasters killed more than 15,000 people.

FACT

Japan is no stranger to earthquakes. In 1923 a 7.9-magnitude quake struck just south of Tokyo. It triggered fires that quickly spread. The earthquake and fires killed more than 140,000 people.

meltdown accident in a nuclear reactor in which the fuel overheats and melts the reactor core or shielding

SURVIVING AN EARTHQUAKE

It's important to be prepared in places where earthquakes can happen. Schoolchildren learn to take shelter under desks or other strong furniture if a quake hits. When outdoors, people should stay away from buildings that could collapse. Staying calm and thinking clearly can help to keep people safe.

DISASTER EMERGENCY KIT

An emergency kit can be very helpful in case of an earthquake. A good kit should include these items:

- ✔ first-aid kit
- ✔ torch
- ✔ battery-powered radio
- ✔ extra batteries
- ✔ blankets
- ✔ bottled water
- ✔ tinned and dried food
- ✔ tin opener
- ✔ whistle to alert rescue workers

GLOSSARY

aftershock smaller earthquake that follows a large one

earthquake sudden shaking of the ground when Earth's crust shifts

epicentre point on Earth's surface directly above the place where an earthquake occurs

fault crack in Earth's crust; earthquakes often occur along faults

landslide large mass of earth and rocks that suddenly slides down a mountain or hill

liquefaction process of soil becoming fluid and unstable during an earthquake

magnitude measure of the size of an earthquake

meltdown accident in a nuclear reactor in which the fuel overheats and melts the reactor core or shielding

province district or a region of some countries

seismic wave movement in the ground created by an earthquake

tsunami large, destructive ocean wave caused by an underwater earthquake, landslide or volcanic eruption

READ MORE

Buried in Rubble: True Tales of Surviving Earthquakes (True Stories of Survival), Terry Collins (Raintree, 2015)

Fearsome Forces of Nature (Extreme Nature), Anita Ganeri (Raintree, 2013)

Surviving Earthquakes (Children's True Stories: Natural Disasters), Michael Burgan (Raintree, 2012)

WEBSITES

www.dkfindout.com/uk/earth/earthquakes

Find out more about what causes earthquakes, and listen to an earth tremor!

ncws.co.uk/cbbcnews/hi/find_out/guides/tech/ earthquakes/newsid_1894000/1894934.stm

Discover more about earthquakes, following news stories from around the world.

COMPREHENSION QUESTIONS

1. Earthquakes are some of the most powerful natural disasters in the world. Which earthquake was the strongest ever recorded? Which one killed the most people in history?

2. Explain what you would do if you were caught in an earthquake.

3. Look at the chart on pages 4–5. What kind of damage can be expected for each level of magnitude on the Richter scale?

INDEX